私のたくさんの色:

ノンバイナリーの物語

Japanese

Marcy Schaaf

When a child expresses a preference to be referred to using "they/them" pronouns, it typically means that they identify as non-binary or genderqueer. Non-binary is a term used to describe individuals whose gender identity doesn't exclusively align with the traditional categories of male or female. Instead, they may experience their gender identity as being somewhere along a spectrum beyond these binary options.

Choosing to use "they/them" pronouns acknowledges and respects the child's gender identity and their right to define themselves in a way that feels authentic to them. It's important to honor their preferred pronouns and provide support and understanding as they navigate their gender identity. This may involve educating others around them, such as family members, friends, and teachers, about the importance of using the correct pronouns and respecting the child's identity.

It's essential to create an environment where the child feels safe and accepted for who they are, regardless of their gender identity. This may involve advocating for inclusive policies and practices in schools, healthcare settings, and other institutions to ensure that non-binary individuals are respected and supported.

子供が「they/them」代名詞で呼ばれることを好む場合、それは通常、その子供がノンバイナリーまたはジェンダークィアであると自認していることを意味します。ノンバイナリーとは、性自認が男性または女性という従来のカテゴリに完全に一致しない個人を表すために使用される用語です。代わりに、彼らは自分の性自認をこれらのバイナリオプションを超えたスペクトルのどこかにあると経験する場合があります。

「they/them」代名詞の使用を選択することは、子供の性自認と、子供が自分らしく感じる方法で自分自身を定義する権利を認め、尊重することになります。子供が好む代名詞を尊重し、子供が性自認を模索する中でサポートと理解を提供することが重要です。これには、家族、友人、教師など、子供の周囲の人々に、正しい代名詞を使用することの重要性と子供のアイデンティティを尊重することについて教育することが含まれる場合があります。

子どもが、自分の性自認に関係なく、安全で、ありのままの自分を受け入れられると感じられる環境を作ることが重要です。これには、学校、医療現場、その他の機関で包括的なポリシーと実践を推進し、ノンバイナリーの個人が尊重され、サポートされるようにすることが含まれる場合があります。

In a small town nestled between rolling hills and whispering forests, there lived a child named Alex.

なだらかな丘とささやく森に囲まれた小さな町に、アレックスという名の子供が住んでいました。

But something else made Alex different too. Some days, they felt as delicate as a butterfly, and on those days, they liked to wear dresses.

しかし、アレックスを他の人と違う
ものにした他の点もありました。あ
る日、彼らは蝶のように繊細だと感
じ、そんな日はドレスを着るのが好
きでした。

Other days, Alex felt strong and bold, like a mighty lion. On those days, they chose pants and shirts that made them feel powerful and free.

別の日には、アレックスは力強いライオンのように、力強く大胆に感じました。そんな日には、彼らは力強く自由な気持ちになれるパンツとシャツを選びました。

But most days, Alex was somewhere in between. They didn't feel entirely like a boy or completely like a girl. They just felt like themselves, a beautiful blend of everything in between.

しかし、ほとんどの日、アレックスはその中間のどこかにいました。完全に男の子のようにも、完全に女の子のようにも感じませんでした。ただ、その中間のすべてが美しく混ざり合った、自分らしさを感じていました。

Some people understood Alex's unique way of being, and they celebrated it with open arms and warm smiles.

アレックスのユニークな生き方を理解し、両手を広げて温かい笑顔で祝福してくれた人もいました。

But others didn't understand. They would stare or whisper, unsure of what to make of someone who didn't fit neatly into their idea of boy or girl.

しかし、他の人たちは理解しませんでした。彼らは、男の子や女の子という自分たちのイメージにうまく当てはまらない人をどう捉えていいのかわからず、じっと見つめたり、ささやいたりしていました。

One day, Alex's grandmother came to visit. She looked puzzled when she saw Alex wearing pants instead of a dress.

ある日、アレックスのおばあちゃんが訪ねてきました。アレックスがドレスではなくズボンを履いているのを見て、おばあちゃんは困惑した様子でした。

"Why aren't you wearing a pretty dress, my dear?" she asked, her voice full of confusion.

「どうしてきれいなドレスを着ていないの？」と彼女は困惑した声で尋ねました。

Alex took a deep breath, feeling nervous but determined to explain. "Sometimes, I feel more like a boy, Grandma. And today is one of those days."

アレックスは深呼吸をして、緊張しながらも説明する決心をしました。「おばあちゃん、時々、僕って男の子みたいに感じることがあるんです。今日はそんな日の一つです。」

Grandma listened carefully,
her eyes softening with
understanding. "Oh, I see,"
she said gently.
"Well, you always look lovely, no
matter what you wear."

おばあちゃんは注意深く聞いて、理解したように目が柔らかくなりました。「ああ、なるほど」と優しく言いました。
「まあ、何を着ても、あなたはいつも素敵ですね。」

As Alex grew older, they learned how to have difficult conversations with teachers, friends, and family members about their gender identity.

she he
they

アレックスが成長するにつれ、彼ら
は教師、友人、家族と性自認について
て難しい会話をする方法を学びまし
た。

she he
they

They discovered that some people would have questions or need time to understand, and that was okay. Patience and kindness were their greatest allies.

彼らは、疑問を持ったり、理解する
のに時間が必要な人もいるが、それ
は問題ないということに気づいた。
忍耐と優しさが彼らの最大の味方だ
った。

And as Alex looked around at the world, they realized that not everyone would understand, and that was okay too. What mattered most was being true to themselves.

　そしてアレックスが世界を見渡すと、誰もが理解してくれるわけではないが、それでも構わないと気づきました。最も大切なのは、自分自身に誠実であることです。

One day, as the sun dipped low in the sky and painted the world with shades of pink and gold, Alex had a realization.

ある日、太陽が低く沈み、世界がピンクと金色の色合いに染まったとき、アレックスはあることに気づきました。

"I may be neither strictly a boy nor only a girl," they thought to themselves, "but I am me. And that is enough."

「私は厳密に言えば男の子でも女の子でもないかもしれない」と彼らは思いました。「でも私は私。それで十分だ」

And so, Alex embraced their uniqueness with pride, knowing that their true colors shone brightest when they were being authentically themselves.

そしてアレックスは、彼らが自分らしくいるときに本当の色が最も輝くことを知り、彼らのユニークさを誇りを持って受け入れました。

The end.

終わり。

Life Lesson:

Embrace your uniqueness and be true to yourself, even if others may not understand. You are beautiful just the way you are.

人生の教訓:
たとえ他の人が理解してくれなくても、自分のユニークさを受け入れて自分に正直になりましょう。あなたはそのままで美しいのです。

Non-binary kids, like anyone else, may have diverse preferences when it comes to how they like to dress. There's no single "right" way for non-binary individuals to dress, as gender expression is highly personal and can vary greatly from person to person. Some non-binary kids may prefer clothing that is traditionally associated with their assigned gender at birth, while others may gravitate towards clothing that blurs or challenges traditional gender norms.

Here are some common ways non-binary kids might choose to dress:

1. Gender-neutral clothing: Many non-binary individuals prefer clothing that is not specifically associated with either traditional gender category. This might include items like t-shirts, jeans, hoodies, sneakers, and other styles that are not inherently gendered.

2. Mix-and-match styles: Some non-binary kids may enjoy mixing elements of traditionally masculine and feminine clothing in their outfits. This could involve wearing clothing from both the men's and women's sections of stores, or combining traditionally masculine and feminine accessories.

3. Androgynous fashion: Androgynous fashion often features clothing styles that blur the lines between masculine and feminine aesthetics. This might include tailored suits, button-up shirts, blazers, skirts, dresses, androgynous hairstyles, and accessories that aren't strongly gendered.

4. Personal expression: Ultimately, non-binary kids may choose to dress in a way that reflects their unique personality, interests, and sense of style. They may experiment with different looks, colors, patterns, and accessories to express themselves authentically.

It's important to respect and support non-binary kids in their clothing choices, just as you would with any child. Creating an inclusive environment where they feel comfortable expressing themselves is key to fostering their confidence and well-being.

ノンバイナリーの子供も、他の子供と同じように、服装に関して多様な好み
を持っている可能性があります。ジェンダー表現は非常に個人的なものであ
り、人によって大きく異なる可能性があるため、ノンバイナリーの個人にと
って「正しい」服装は一つではありません。ノンバイナリーの子供の中に
は、生まれたときに割り当てられた性別と伝統的に関連付けられている服装
を好む子供もいれば、伝統的な性別の規範を曖昧にしたり挑戦したりする服
装に惹かれる子供もいます。

ノンバイナリーの子供たちが選ぶ一般的な服装は以下のとおりです。

1. ジェンダーニュートラルな服: 多くのノンバイナリーの人は、伝統的なジェ
ンダーのカテゴリーに特に関連しない服を好みます。これには、Tシャツ、ジ
ーンズ、パーカー、スニーカー、その他、本質的にジェンダー化されていな
いスタイルのアイテムが含まれます。

2. ミックスアンドマッチスタイル: ノンバイナリーの子供の中には、伝統的な
男性服と女性服の要素を服装にミックスすることを楽しむ子もいます。これ
には、店の男性用と女性用の両方のセクションの服を着たり、伝統的な男性
用と女性用のアクセサリーを組み合わせたりすることが含まれます。

3. 両性具有のファッション: 両性具有のファッションは、男性的な美学と女性
的な美学の境界線を曖昧にする服装スタイルを特徴とすることが多いです。
これには、仕立てられたスーツ、ボタンアップシャツ、ブレザー、スカー
ト、ドレス、両性具有のヘアスタイル、性別があまりはっきりしないアクセ
サリーなどが含まれます。

4. 個人の表現: 最終的には、ノンバイナリーの子供たちは、自分独自の個性、
興味、スタイル感覚を反映した服装を選ぶかもしれません。彼らは、本物の
自分を表現するため、さまざまな外見、色、パターン、アクセサリーを試す
かもしれません。

他の子どもと同じように、ノンバイナリーの子どもの服装の選択を尊重し、
サポートすることが重要です。子どもが安心して自分を表現できる包括的な
環境を作ることが、子どもの自信と幸福を育む鍵となります。

Hey there, colorful kids! Have you ever wondered how to pick the perfect colors for your outfit? It's easy! Just think about how you're feeling and what outfit you want to wear. If you're feeling as bright as a sunny day, maybe choose clothes in vibrant yellows and oranges. Or if you're feeling calm and peaceful, soft blues and greens might be just the right colors for you. Let your outfit be your canvas and your feelings be your guide as you paint the world with your unique style and personality!

　カラフルな子供たちの皆さん、こんにちは！服装にぴったりの色を選ぶ方法を考えたことがありますか？簡単です！気分や着たい服装について考えてみてください。晴れた日のように明るい気分なら、鮮やかな黄色やオレンジ色の服を選ぶといいでしょう。または、穏やかで平和な気分なら、淡い青や緑がぴったりの色かもしれません。服装をキャンバスに、気持ちをガイドにして、独自のスタイルと個性で世界を描きましょう！

Explore these pages to discover your unique style.

これらのページを探索して、独自の
スタイルを見つけてください。

My Many Colors:
A Story of Being Non-Binary

My Non-Binary Coloring Book

$10
on our website

Marcy Schaaf

Join Our Book of the Month Club!

Looking for the perfect gift that keeps on giving? Join our Book of the Month Club! For just $25 a month, or $250 if you purchase a year upfront, you or your loved ones will receive a handpicked children's book every month, straight to your doorstep.

Here's how it works:
Choose from 15 different languages to receive bilingual books that make learning fun.
Enjoy monthly shipments of our exclusive books that inspire, teach, and entertain children of all ages.
Each month's book is carefully selected to provide a new adventure, valuable lesson, and a chance to explore cultures from around the world.
It's the perfect gift for birthdays, holidays, or just because! Whether you're nurturing a young reader or encouraging language learning, our Book of the Month Club is designed to bring joy to every bookshelf.

Exclusive Bonus: As part of your membership, you'll also receive a monthly podcast about our featured book delivered straight to your email! Listen in for behind-the-scenes insights, fun facts, and tips for making storytime even more magical.

Sign up today at www.Booksbyschaaf.com and start enjoying the gift of reading all year long!

今月のブッククラブにご参加ください!

ずっと贈り続けられる完璧なギフトをお探しですか? 弊社の Book of the Month Club にご参加ください! 月額わずか 25 ドル、または 1 年分を前払いで購入する場合は 250 ドルで、あなたやあなたの大切な人に毎月、厳選された子供向けの本が直接ご自宅に届きます。

仕組みは次のとおりです:
15 種類の言語から選択して、楽しく学習できるバイリンガル ブックを受け取ります。
あらゆる年齢の子供たちに刺激を与え、教育し、楽しませる当社の独占書籍を毎月お届けします。
毎月の本は、新しい冒険、貴重な教訓、そして世界中の文化を探索する機会を提供するために慎重に選ばれています。
誕生日や休日、または何気ないお祝いにもぴったりのギフトです。幼い読書を育てたり、言語学習を奨励したりする場合でも、当社の Book of the Month Club は、すべての本棚に喜びをもたらすように設計されています。

限定特典: メンバーシップの一環として、特集本に関するポッドキャストを毎月メールで直接お届けします。舞台裏の洞察、楽しい事実、ストーリータイムをさらに魔法のようにするヒントをお聞きください。

今すぐ www.Booksbyschaaf.com にサインアップして、一年中読書の楽しみを楽しみましょう。

Books By Schaaf

www.BookBySchaaf.com

Podcast series about our book on TikTok.

Activity Guide companion's for each storybook can be found on our website.

Find us at: